Dedication

Thank you God for blessing and guiding me. This book is dedi⸺ ⸻ ⸻ ⸻
have helped me become a better, stronger, more resilient, and more intelligent woman.

Acknowledgments

Illustrated by: Julie J Sheah
Website: https://www.behance.net/juliegoesnuts

Edited by: Amelia S. Bugst

You Can Find Cupid's Planner at:

www.cupidsplanner.com
Facebook: www.facebook/cupidsplanner
Twitter: www.twitter.com/cupidsplanner
Instagram: www.instagram/cupidsplanner
Email: Cupid@cupidsplanner.com

Disclaimer

A special thank you to my big sister, LaRaya Davis Cray, for contributing a poem and always encouraging me.

Self

When looking in the mirror
Remember to find your inner
and to listen and hear the whisper.
Always strive and dive in this lifetime to survive
Let your spirit know you have arrived
Show love and allow it to bloom like rosebuds.
Open up your heart as big as the skies and showing self how high
as you think about the birds and how they were meant to fly
in the wind passing us by.
Love your family
as it grows rapidly
while being happily engaged.
Always knowing this was something that was named,
Love for family won't be changed.
Live today with no regrets and don't forget to always look back and reflect on life events.

~ LaRaya Davis Cray

The Man Behind the Woman: A Tribute to My Father

They say behind every strong man is an even stronger woman, although I believe that behind every strong woman is a loving father. Now, this is not to say that women who did not grow up with a father are not strong. But there *is* something inarticulately special about a father's love and the bond he shares with his daughter. Every daddy's girl will understand this connection and will know just how hard it is to put into words. Through a father's love, a daughter learns so many simple yet crucial truths that affirm and strengthen her sense of dignity and self-worth. A father's unwavering love helps his daughter learn important life lessons about forming healthy attachments, and his support helps her discover the treatment she deserves from the opposite gender. But perhaps most importantly, a father's love is the cushion a daughter sometimes needs to fall back against when her self-worth quivers or when other people in her life inevitably let her down. With that said, here are three truths I learned from my father, three truths that have shaped me into the strong, courageous, and independent woman I so appreciatively am today.

"Be a strong, independent woman. Do not depend on no man. Always be able to take care of yourself."

My father is a simple, hardworking man who prides himself on taking care of and providing for his family. Although he is not a rich man, he has filled my life with a wealth of knowledge and wisdom. My father began sharing his exceptional advice with me at an early age. His advice, permanently ingrained in the forefront of my mind, has taught me the importance of being independent, which ignited and fueled my desire to pursue a higher education and start my own business. His advice is what drives me, inspires me, and motivates my every thought and action. My father's advice has followed me throughout my childhood and into adulthood, and it is what keeps me going when times are tough.

"Do not worry about what everyone else is doing. If you feel it is the right thing to do, do it! Do not be bullied into silence."

My father consistently reminded me of this piece of advice throughout my childhood. As an impressionable young girl, my father's advice encouraged me, even pushed me, to treat others kindly, even when I thought they did not deserve it. As an adult, my father's advice still lingers: when people ask for my opinion, I tell them. I do not say things to fit in, even if it means being criticized and ostracized for standing by my values. His words have served me greatly because they prompt me to be a woman of my word, to strive for kindness, and to always act considerately and honestly. To this day my father's words continue to stimulate my desire to be a woman of steadfast compassion, kindness, and integrity.

"Sometimes you have to take a little shit to get what you want."

Much of the advice my father gave to me came from his own life experiences, and at some point in his life, he came to realize that you sometimes have to take a little shit to get what you want. Taking grief to achieve greatness is an unpleasant but necessary part of life. Fortunately, my father's advice spared me from finding this truth out the hard, disappointing way. My father shared his personal realizations with me knowing full well that my ambitious, straightforward, determined, and no-nonsense personality would need it. Our father-daughter bond allowed him to understand my disinterest in playing games and my aversion to being disingenuous. He understood me in a way no one else could, so he gave me this advice to help ease the disappointments I would come across when others failed to mirror my own no-nonsense attitude and ambitious as well as determined personality. In return, I learned humility, perseverance, resilience, and how to focus on my goals. I use my father's invaluable lesson to brush aside failure, to get back up when I stumble, and to confront adversity yet again. Through my conversations with my father, I have learned that being a unique individual is perfectly okay. I have learned and accepted that I do not need to be like everyone or anyone else.

My father neither babied me nor called me princess. Instead, he equipped me with practical, tangible advice that has helped mold me into a woman of strength, compassion, integrity, and courage. I have carried his advice with me since I was a child. And it has shaped me into the woman I am today and will forever act as my personal guide.

The Acknowledgment

It was me looking back at me,
Inquiring my mind about the reflection I see.

Rebellious times twinkling in my eyes
While I selfishly reminisce.
I wonder, who is this brown-eyed, brown-faced girl?

Girl?

While the warmth of the rising sun tickles my skin,
It eclipses on my savorless fun.
The melted caramel mold of the curvaceous woman I see,
Transmitting energy and exuding radiance.

The woman I see?

Making my footprint, I take the first step.
Praying on my knees,
I faithfully walk but sinfully live,
Stumbling on a tightrope

The Lord forgives me.

I struggle to define the brown eyes and brown face reflecting back at me
But I smile.
It is me!

Missing You

Missing you because you are one of the few
Who are true,
True to my heart.

Missing you because you are so dear to me
Gone and left without a goodbye
How rude?

Missing you because there is no sight or scent of you
There is no touch that can be felt.

Missing you because I love you
I yearn to be near you.

I miss you a ton, with all of my heart.

I miss you.

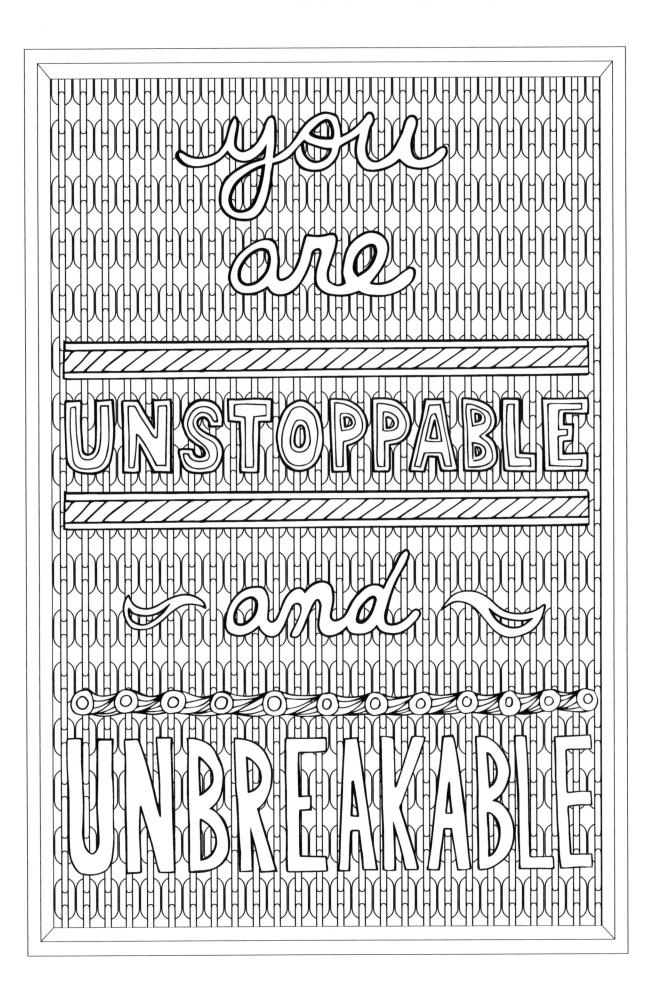

Tuesday

Birds tweeting
Air whisking against my cheeks
Rays peeking into my window
A fight ensues with the sun
Mr. Sunshine is a persistent son of a bitch
Yearning to sink deeper into my king-sized sheets
A rooster crows
A 15-minute snooze rapidly dissipates
I think, so many things to do today
My ungrateful boss
A boring lunch
Nosy coworkers
Traffic lights
Horns blaring
Is it Friday, yet?
Gradually
I rise out of my bed
Stretch my neck
Rotate my shoulders
And I praise the Lord for another day

A Man-eater

I thought it was true love
The sight of him, the ebony-eyed boy
His chocolate skin
Ripped muscles, luring me in

I thought it was true love
His chest against mine
Vibrations through my spine and down my thighs
Cries to high heavens, what a delightful surprise

I thought it was true love
Ebony eyes gazing into mine
Thoughtlessly snuggling him
Dreaming of a place with just me and him
A house in the suburbs and a white picket fence

I thought it was true love
He almost checked my list
And then I saw another one

A better one

And I thought it was true love

A Legacy of Strong Women: Lessons Learned from my Grandmothers

I used to be surprised when people described me as strong and courageous. I often did not feel this way, especially when life's challenges and setbacks seemed to trip me up, knock me over, and bring me down. But regardless of how hard life hit me or the height of the hurdles I had to overcome, I always found a way to get back up. Knowing God has my back allowed me to do this. Without him, I would be nothing! However, I have recently realized that my resilience and ability to overcome challenges comes from another source as well - I come from a legacy of strong women.

I was fortunate as a child to have both of my grandmothers. My maternal grandmother was too sassy and cool to be called Grandmom, so we called her Momma Connie. Momma Connie's strong and lively personality would always come through as we watched Jerry Springer and ate cheesesteaks, her sassy yet equally hilarious comments always filling momentary silences. My paternal grandmother was more of a traditional grandmother, so we simply called her Grandma. She could cook anything and would talk about everybody. She cracked me up. My grandmothers were very different from each other, yet both readily voiced their opinions and freely spoke their mind – we never knew what they might say because they were bound to say anything. They would speak the truth and let you know exactly how they felt. I have always admired this about them.

The memories I have of my grandmothers and the lessons they taught me throughout my life are still with me. I remember one day, I made a mistake and I frantically apologized to Momma Connie about it. She told me, "You do not need to say sorry. You do not need to apologize for anything!" On that day, I not only learned that I was entitled to make mistakes, but that I also did not need to apologize for them. Now, I am not saying I am reckless, but I am not going to beat myself up for moments of temporary failure, nor am I going to criticize myself for making minor mistakes. I try not to be too hard on myself because plenty of people in this world are ready to do that for me. Although I learned from Momma Connie not to criticize myself for the ups and downs of daily life, I am not always successful at doing so. Like many others, I am often my own worst critic. But, when I start to feel self-pity or think poorly about myself, I hear Momma's voice telling me, "You don't have to apologize for anything!"

While Momma Connie taught me not to apologize for my innocent mistakes, Grandma showed me the importance of not being bound by social norms and stigmas. Grandma was in an abusive marriage for many years, but once she decided the time was right, she left. She did not let society dictate who she was, who she should be married to, or the treatment she should tolerate in her marriage. She defined and set her own standards and boundaries. She embarked on and embraced the journey of being a single woman despite the stigmatization of divorce in her time. Her self-worth was something I, as a young girl, watched her continuously demonstrate through her audacity to be a woman of undeniable courage, admirable independence, and unwavering fortitude. Being the impressionable and adoring granddaughter I was, I witnessed and learned important life lessons from Grandma's experiences. Her experience in an unhealthy marriage has guided my own views and opinions of relationships. I will not be in a relationship just for the sake of being in one! In essence, Grandma's personal experiences have taught me just how crucial it is to enter a relationship with someone who not only complements my mind, body, and soul, but who also helps me become a better and stronger woman.

The memories, life lessons, and words of wisdom I have from my grandmothers frequently cross my mind, especially when I am having a difficult day or when I struggle to find the best course of action. In these moments, I often find myself asking, "What would Momma Connie say? What would Grandma do?" Asking myself these questions during difficult times has been life changing since both of my grandmothers were forces of nature who danced to their own drumbeat. Using the memories I have of my grandmothers has allowed me to become an equally independent and strong woman who also dances to her own, uniquely dynamic drumbeat.

Momma Connie and Grandma taught me exceptionally wise, priceless life lessons that have shaped me into the unique woman I am today. They also taught me the simplest of life lessons that I eagerly embrace each and every day: how to make potato salad, how to bake a pound cake, how to tell somebody off, how not to back down from a fight, how to subtly read someone, and how to be a strong, brave, and courageous woman.

Because of my grandmothers, I wake up every day knowing I was not built to break. I wake up every day knowing that I come from a strong background. I wake up every day thankful that I come from a legacy of strong women.

The Disillusioned One

He was six foot five with cold black eyes.
Walking into my life with a stride of confidence and a touch of arrogance.
His legs smoothly danced me around to my favorite song.
While his brazen arms twirled me to the beat.
His chiseled chest comforted me while I attempted to forget my fears.
His hands caressed my neck, earnestly awakening me.
His eyes sparkled an untold story of love, *and I believed.*

But it was his lips that broke my heart.

To Receive LOVE IS GREAT BUT TO GIVE LOVE IS EVEN BETTER

My Ryde or Die Chick: A Tribute to My Mother

My mother loves me despite my flaws and supports me through all my endeavors, encourages me to move forward when my self-esteem wavers, and most importantly, accepts me for who I am.

People may say all of these actions are what a mother is naturally supposed to do, but my mother's love is a *special kind of love*. It is a special kind of love that has taken root deep down in both our souls. It is a special kind of love that knows me in and out, a love that can tell when I am hurt, sad, happy, or mad by the slightest change in my facial expression. It is a special kind of love that always keeps me in mind, whether I'm in the next room over or far away for extended periods of time. It is a special kind of love that can make you think you are rich even when you are broke. It is a special kind of love that, through many sacrifices, never weakens and only grows stronger. It is a special kind of love that fuses together my mother's traditional role and my unconventional ways, allowing us to meet at a mutual place of understanding and respect. It is a special kind of love that forgives me even when I am a brat, like that time when I was about five years old and my mother took me to Payless, to Ames, and all around Langley Park looking for purple and pink snow boots because I just *had* to have those specific colors. I felt so rich and special, but that was simply my mother's love. My mother's love is a truly rare love that, despite what I have written here, is difficult to put into words. It is a love that I receive only from my mother. It is a special kind of love that exists only between a loving mother and her admiring daughter.

My mother's unshakeable love has taught me to live life like a force of nature: to be bold, honest, and unapologetic for being E.B. Throughout my highs and lows, I know I have a personal fan who will encourage me no matter what the circumstances and a cheerleader who will lift me up and dust me off when I fall down. I am thankful to have such an amazing, compassionate woman in my life who knows how and when to be both a caring mom and a faithful friend. She is inextricably a mother and a best friend, the one person I know will *always* have my back. She is my Ryde or Die Chick!

Through My Worst

Through my messy hair
He sees my beauty

Through my growing waistline
He feels my curves

Through my fits of raging terror
He hears my cries to be understood

Through my moments of solitude
He respects my mood

Through my pitiful bits of failure
He tastes the success that manifests through my lips

Through the yellow and blue
He is never too far away

I am at my best, even through my worst, because of him

Family

My mother made me with her strength and beauty, and my father breathed life into me with his loyalty, hard work, and stubbornness.

 They keep me sane by telling me how it is.

My sisters are my secret whisper-keepers, and my cousins are my first best friends.

 They are my soldiers when it is time to go to war.

My nieces show me how to love unconditionally, and my nephews are the boys who keep a smile on my face.

 They show me tenderness in this harsh, cruel world.

My aunts show me compassion and friendship, and my uncles give me cheer.

 They keep me encouraged.

My grandmothers tell me to defy boundaries and show me how to break down walls with their spirit of courage. My grandfathers speak wisdom into my footsteps, one at a time.

 They give me a legacy of character greater than silver or gold.

I did not ask for them.
They were given to me by God to help me be a better me.

The Things in the Night

There are certain things that keep me up at night.

These are the things that make me shiver with regret
And fill me with unspoken assumptions
Retaliated with misspoken words and misplaced feelings
Grappled with the fury of red

These are the things that go bump in the night
A bruised fate and an undiscovered destiny
Bursting with greatness
But lingering with self-doubt and uncertainty
Until I am green in the face with the ordinary

These are the things that creep throughout the night
Walking slowly up my bed sheets, silkening my skin
Reminding me that I am alone
Dreaming of adulterated love
These are the things that cause me to awaken brokenhearted
And reanimate my courageous existence
Auspiciously mending the pieces – back again
I am reminded of the things that keep me up at night

While I am up at night.

A Little Bit of Courage

And suddenly she exhaled, realizing she was not built to break
Roaming a land of unbeknownst challenges,
Thrills, paranoia, and fears
She roamed bravely!

She roamed boldly
Tackling and tickling her fancy
She roamed because she knew who she was
Conquering and devouring the tiny little voice in her head that says she can't
With the courage of her heartbeat that pumps I can

She breathed in the possibilities
Exhaling the toxins of past hurts, pains, disappointments, doubts, and shame
And inhaling optimism, gratitude, courage, and empathy
Holding it in
Absorbing it into every limb
Morphing herself into a triumphant woman

She was not built to break
She was made out of lion's skin
She released the spirit of fear
And roared *World, here I come!*

Then the roar turned into a snore
And daylight faded into darkness
If not today then tomorrow

Sometimes the day wins the fight
But she was not built to break
And so she exhaled

The True Beauty of Friendship

We all have friends – friends we grew up with, friends we played tag with, and friends who stayed over at our houses so often they simply became a part of the family. We have had friends who turned into enemies, friendships that slowly drifted away, and special people in our lives who we are so fortunate to call our friends today. It is funny how one day you can meet someone who changes your life forever, simply because they bring out either the best or the worst in you.

As I reflect on my childhood friendships and current adult friendships, I can say that I understand the true value of friendship. Friends are the caring and supportive family members you choose. They are the exceptional people you willingly and eagerly surround yourself with, the ones you turn to for advice during your darkest moments, and the amazing people who, no matter what, have your back. In fact, I honestly do not know what I would do without my girl-talk time with my one-of-a-kind, caring, understanding, and supportive friends. Although it is often difficult to explain just how much my friends truly mean to me, I have tried to put it into words.

My friends are the friends you can call in the middle of the night and cry to.

They are the friends who would willingly drag themselves out of bed to pick you up in the middle of the night because your car broke down.

They are the friends who know you cannot afford to hang out, but because they enjoy your company so much, they treat you.

They are the friends who are there when you act like a psychotic maniac and are still there when your meltdown is over because they love you in *all* your forms.

They are the friends who will give you guidance when they see you going in the wrong direction, and they will never say "I told you so" if you do eventually make that mistake.

They are the friends who do not let other people talk bad about you and will set someone straight if they do.

They are the friends who can see your ex with someone else and confirm that you look better than his new girlfriend.

They are the friends who let you see them in their most vulnerable moments and do not pretend to be someone they are not.

They are the friends who will hold your hair back when you are throwing up after getting too drunk from a fun night out.

They are the friends who can hang around your crazy family without making any judgments.

They are the friends who will take fifty selfies with you until you get the right one.

They are the friends you argue with one minute and go to the mall with five minutes later, with no animosity whatsoever.

They are the friends who can laugh at you *and* laugh with you because sometimes you are just silly.

Through the many friendships I have had throughout my life, I have realized that many people and things come and go. I have learned that a genuine friendship does not depend on how long you have known a person, or on how frequently you talk to that person. A true friend accepts you for who you are, no matter the situation. I have realized that a true friend does not stop being your friend because they have experienced some major life-changing event. They do not stop being your friend because they got married and you are still single, and they do not stop being your friend because they have children and you do not. They do not stop being your friend because you can no longer do favors for them, they do not stop being your friend because you moved away, and they do not stop being your friend because you have different political views or opinions. True friends do not judge your past, but see the greatness of your future. They recognize that you are a unique individual, and they simply enjoy spending time with you. These types of friends are very rare. They are true diamonds that bring endless light, radiance, and beauty into your life – into *my* life.

A Better Me!

Who, me?
No, that was not me!
You're tripping.
Oh, that?
Right.
It was not like that.
I told you the truth.
I am not lying, baby.
I do not know what you are talking about.
But baby!
But baby!
You are still talking about that?
Why are you bringing up the past?
But I love you, sweetpea.
I don't love her.
What are you talking about?
Who would you be without me?
I love you.
You love me!
We were meant to be.
It will not happen again.
I promise!?
Forgive me.
Baby.

And then I let go and found a better me!

surround yourself
WITH
PEOPLE WHO
ENCOURAGE
YOUR
SPIRIT

Made in the USA
Middletown, DE
18 May 2016